only *1* thing

KENNETH COPELAND

JESUS IS LORD

KENNETH COPELAND
PUBLICATIONS

Unless otherwise noted, all scripture is from the *King James Version* of the Bible.

Scripture quotations marked *The Amplified Bible* are from *The Amplified Bible, Old Testament* © 1965, 1987 by the Zondervan Corporation. *The Amplified New Testament* © 1958, 1987 by The Lockman Foundation. Used by permission.

Only One Thing

ISBN 978-1-60463-089-3
30-0078

25 24 23 22 21 20   7 6 5 4 3 2

© 2013 Eagle Mountain International Church Inc. aka Kenneth Copeland Ministries

Kenneth Copeland Publications
Fort Worth, TX 76192-0001

For more information about Kenneth Copeland Ministries, visit kcm.org or call 1-800-600-7395 (U.S. only) or +1-817-852-6000.

only 1 *thing*

Think how great it would be if you had only one thing on your to-do list today.

Not 100.

Not 10.

Just one.

One thing that would put you and keep you in the perfect will of

God, that would guarantee your success, and empower you to be BLESSED and a BLESSING every day of your life.

Sounds great, doesn't it? But to most people (Christians included) it also sounds too good to be true. "My life is complicated and demanding," they say. "I have to earn a living. I have to take care of my family and fulfill my responsibilities at church. I have a lot of different priorities. I can't tend to just one thing!"

From the world's perspective, such statements make sense. But according to the Bible, that's not how God sees it. He says we have just one priority: "My son, attend to my words" (Proverbs 4:20).

What does it mean to attend to God's WORD? It means we put it first and make it final authority in our spirit, soul, body, finances and everything we do every day. It means we set our attention on The WORD seven days a week, day in and day out, month after month. It means we always take time to hear what The LORD is telling us so we can say and do whatever He tells us to.

In short, it means we hang on Jesus' every word.

"But Brother Copeland, I'm too busy," you might say.

That's what Martha thought, too. Remember her story? She's the woman in Luke 10 who hosted one of Jesus' teaching meetings in her home.

If anyone ever had reason to think she didn't have time for The WORD, Martha did. Especially the day Jesus came to her house. He had His 12 disciples with Him, and who knows how many of His other 70 staff members. Needless to say, Martha was very busy! She was not only playing hostess to a virtual multitude, she was trying to figure out how to keep them fed.

She didn't have the luxury of calling Colonel Sanders to deliver meals for everyone like we do, today. She had to make everything. Initially she assumed her sister Mary would help, but Mary threw her a curve. Instead of heading for the kitchen, Mary joined the disciples, "sat at Jesus' feet, and heard his word" (verse 39).

So while Jesus taught and everyone else listened, Martha tended to the business of cooking...all by herself.

And she wasn't happy about it. *This just isn't right!* she thought. *I'm out here in the kitchen working as hard as I can, and that lazy sister of mine is sitting in there at the preacher's feet. She ought to be helping me.*

Finally, Martha couldn't stand it anymore. Convinced Jesus should correct the situation, she marched in and interrupted His sermon. "Lord, dost thou not care that my sister hath left me to serve alone?" she asked. "Bid her therefore that she help me" (verse 40).

All Messed Up With Too Many Things to Do

Imagine this! Not only did Martha make a scene right in the middle of Jesus' meeting, she as much as accused Him of not caring about her. Then she actually told Him what to do.

Most of us can't remember the last time we ordered Jesus around. We know better. But Martha was all messed up. "Overly occupied and too busy...distracted with much serving" (verse 40, *The Amplified Bible*), she had too many things on her to-do list.

How did Jesus help her? He answered and said to her: "Martha,

Martha, thou art careful and troubled about many things: But one thing is needful: and Mary hath chosen that good part, which shall not be taken away from her" (verses 41-42).

To Martha's credit, she didn't argue with what Jesus told her. She didn't say, "Be practical, LORD! What am I supposed to do? Just let everyone go hungry?"

That's how most Christians these days would have responded. But the fact is, Jesus didn't say anything about people going hungry. What He said was that only one thing is needed: to hear and obey His WORD.

When we make that one thing our priority, everything else falls in line.

Martha should have known. After all, she'd heard about the multitudes who'd spent days listening to Jesus preach out on the Galilean hillside. They didn't have anyone cooking meals for them. But they got fed— Jesus made sure of it. He multiplied a little boy's lunch until it was more than enough to feed 20,000 people.

What do you think would have happened if Martha had followed that example? What if she'd walked out of her kitchen with a big bowl of beans, slid them over in front of Jesus, and said, "Sir, I'm not going to miss hearing the living WORD of Almighty God when it's being preached right here in my house. So if You want this bunch to have anything to eat, I trust You'll take care of it. You fed

20,000 with a few loaves and fish. You can certainly feed this houseful of people with these beans!"

Clearly, if Martha had chosen that attitude, if hearing and acting on The WORD had been the only thing on her to-do list that day, everything would have turned out just fine. One way or another, Jesus would have seen to it that everyone had plenty to eat.

The Teacher Is in Your House

"But Brother Copeland," you might say, "Martha's situation was different than mine. Jesus was right there with her, teaching God's WORD!"

Yes, He was. But the same is true for you. As a Holy-Ghost baptized believer, you can sit down, open your Bible and hear Jesus preach to you every day. Why? Because you not only have God's written WORD to read, you have the Holy Spirit living inside you to quicken that WORD and fulfill the promise Jesus made in John 16: "When he, the Spirit of truth, is come, he will guide you into all truth: for he shall not speak of himself; but whatsoever he shall hear, that shall he speak: and he will show you things to come. He shall glorify me: for he shall receive of mine, and shall show it unto you. All things that the Father hath are mine: therefore said I, that he shall take of mine, and shall show [or declare] it unto you" (verses 13-15).

In other words, just like Martha, you have the Teacher in your house —and every day He is saying the same thing to you He said to her: The one thing you really need to do is hear and obey God's WORD.

I can assure you, Jesus isn't saying this because He's oblivious to everything else you have to do. He's saying it because He knows that life itself—all real, genuine life—life for your spirit, for your soul, your body, your family, your finances and everything else— comes from The WORD. As Proverbs 4:22 says, "[God's WORDS] are life unto those that find them, and health to all their flesh."

It's no wonder Jesus wants us to make His WORD our sole priority! That WORD is the force behind all creation. It keeps everything operating. (See Hebrews 1:3.) Nothing works without God's WORD!

Think about it for a moment.

- In the beginning when God created the heavens and the earth, He did it with His WORD. He said, "Let there be light: and there was light" (Genesis 1:3).

- When He made and BLESSED mankind, He did it with His WORD.

He said, "Be fruitful, and multiply, and replenish the earth, and subdue it: and have dominion..." (verse 28).

- When Adam's sin robbed mankind of THE BLESSING and God wanted to restore it, once again He did it with His WORD. "I will bless thee," He said to Abram, "and make thy name great; and thou shalt be a blessing" (Genesis 12:2).

- Even the plan of redemption was brought about by God's WORD. He spoke it to and through prophets, generation after generation, until as John 1 says, "[Jesus] The WORD was made flesh, and dwelt among us," (verse 14); and "as many as received him, to them gave he power to become the sons of God" (verse 12).

16

The Secret to 100% Success

God's WORDs are the foundation of everything in His kingdom. They don't just carry information, and they're not only a means of communication. They're infused with the very power of God Himself.

That's why in John 6:63, Jesus said His WORDs are "spirit, and they are life."

Everything Jesus accomplished in the Gospels, He did by hearing and acting on God's WORD. It's how He operated every day. He attended to The WORD and heard what His Father was saying. Then He said whatever the Father told

Him to say, did whatever the Father told Him to do and God's power came on the scene.

"The WORDS that I speak unto you I speak not of myself," He said, "but the Father that dwelleth in me, he doeth the works" (John 14:10).

Consider the incident at the pool of Bethesda. The Bible tells us that when Jesus walked up to that pool, multitudes of blind, crippled and diseased people were crowded all around waiting for the angel to stir the water. Yet Jesus walked right past them all and focused His attention on one bedridden man. "Wilt thou be made whole?" He asked. "Rise, take up thy bed, and walk" (John 5:6, 8).

Twelve words. That's all Jesus

spoke because that's all the Father told Him to say. As a result, He had 100-percent success. Immediately the man was made whole. Then Jesus walked away.

You know as well as I do, if we'd been there when that man got healed, we wouldn't have done what Jesus did. We would have set up the Pool of Bethesda Healing Association. We would have bottled the water, lined up all the sick people and anointed them with it.

But none of it would have done any good because only one thing is needful. The WORD of God.

Whatever He says, that's what we need to say and do—and nothing else!

The Power That Unlocked Hell

"You just don't understand the kind of problems I'm facing," someone might say. "They're too big to be solved by something as simple as God's WORD."

That's impossible! For your problems to be too big for God's WORD, they'd have to be worse than the ones Jesus faced when He went to the cross, and no one has ever dealt with anything like that.

On the cross, Jesus suffered more than any man ever has. He bore the entire penalty for the sin of all mankind! Although Jesus Himself had never sinned, He was made to be sin

21

for us so that we could receive His righteousness. He "became obedient unto death" (Philippians 2:8) so that we could be set free.

That meant He had to die not just physically but spiritually. He had to take our place, go down into the bowels of this earth to the bottomless pit and spend three days in the very guts of the horrible place called hell. It's not a place created for men. It was created for the devil and his angels.

When Jesus went there every demon in that pit tore into Him. They fully expected to annihilate Him and keep Him there forever. They had good reason to believe they'd be able to do it, too. After all, no one had ever gotten out of hell. The place is locked. It looked like Jesus was trapped there for eternity.

But then something happened.

God's voice came booming out of heaven and cut through that demonic darkness. "Thou art my Son, this day have I begotten thee," He said to Jesus. "Thy throne, O God, is for ever and ever: a sceptre of righteousness is the sceptre of thy kingdom" (Hebrews 1:5, 8).

Those words were spirit and life! When Jesus heard them and put His faith in them, His emaciated, death-wracked spirit was born again. He came alive, rose up in the very likeness of the living God, spoiled principalities and powers, triumphed over them, took the keys of hell and left Satan stripped of everything he had.

Jesus left the devil with absolutely nothing! Then He ascended on high, led captivity captive, gave gifts to men, and made us His joint heirs.

What made it all possible?

The WORD of God!

Don't you think if God's WORD can do all that, it can supply enough divine wisdom, power and life to conquer any challenge you might be facing? Of course it can!

So make it *your* priority. Simplify your life and make attending to God's WORD the only thing on your to-do list. Spend time with Him every day and find out what He's saying to you. Then stick with His plan. Say whatever He tells you to say and do whatever He tells you to do.

It's the only sure way to live BLESSED.

Prayer for Salvation and Baptism in the Holy Spirit

Heavenly Father, I come to You in the Name of Jesus. Your Word says, "Whosoever shall call on the name of the Lord shall be saved" (Acts 2:21). I am calling on You. I pray and ask Jesus to come into my heart and be Lord over my life according to Romans 10:9-10: "If thou shalt confess with thy mouth the Lord Jesus, and shalt believe in thine heart that God hath raised him from the dead, thou shalt be saved. For with the heart man believeth unto righteousness; and with the mouth confession is made unto salvation." I do that now. I confess that Jesus is Lord, and I believe in my heart that God raised Him from the dead. I repent of sin. I renounce it. I renounce the devil and everything he stands for. Jesus is my Lord.

I am now reborn! I am a Christian—a child of Almighty God! I am saved! You also said in Your Word, "If ye then, being evil, know how to give good gifts unto your children: HOW MUCH MORE shall your heavenly Father give the Holy Spirit to them that ask him?" (Luke 11:13). I'm also asking You to fill me with the Holy Spirit. Holy Spirit, rise up within me as I praise God. I fully expect to speak with other tongues as You give me the utterance (Acts 2:4). In Jesus' Name. Amen!

Begin to praise God for filling you with the Holy Spirit. Speak those words and syllables you receive—not in your own language, but the language given to you by the Holy Spirit. You have to use your own voice. God will not force you to speak. Don't be concerned with how it sounds. It is a heavenly language!

Continue with the blessing God has given you and pray in the spirit every day.

You are a born-again, Spirit-filled believer. You'll never be the same!

Find a good church that boldly preaches God's Word and obeys it. Become part of a church family who will love and care for you as you love and care for them.

We need to be connected to each other. It increases our strength in God. It's God's plan for us.

Make it a habit to watch the Believer's Voice of Victory Network and become a doer of the Word, who is blessed in his doing (James 1:22-25).

About the Author

Kenneth Copeland is co-founder and president of Kenneth Copeland Ministries in Fort Worth, Texas, and best-selling author of books that include *Honor—Walking in Honesty, Truth and Integrity*, and *THE BLESSING of The LORD Makes Rich and He Adds No Sorrow With It*.

Since 1967, Kenneth has been a minister of the gospel of Christ and teacher of God's WORD. He is also the artist on award-winning albums such as his Grammy-nominated *Only the Redeemed, In His Presence, He Is Jehovah, Just a Closer Walk* and *Big Band Gospel*. He also co-stars as the character Wichita Slim in the children's adventure videos *The Gunslinger, Covenant Rider* and the movie *The Treasure of Eagle Mountain*, and as Daniel Lyon in the Commander Kellie and the Superkids™ videos *Armor of Light* and *Judgment: The Trial of Commander Kellie*. Kenneth also co-stars as a Hispanic godfather in the 2009 and 2016 movies *The Rally* and *The Rally 2: Breaking the Curse*.

With the help of offices and staff in the United States, Canada, England, Australia, South Africa, Ukraine and Latin America, Kenneth is fulfilling his vision to boldly preach the uncompromised WORD of God from the top of the world, to the bottom, and all the way around the middle. His ministry reaches millions of people worldwide through daily and Sunday TV broadcasts, magazines, teaching audios and videos, conventions and campaigns, and the World Wide Web.

Learn more about Kenneth Copeland Ministries by visiting our website at **kcm.org.**

When the Lord first spoke to Kenneth and Gloria Copeland about starting the *Believer's Voice of Victory* magazine...

He said: *This is your seed. Give it to everyone who ever responds to your ministry, and don't ever allow anyone to pay for a subscription!*

For more than 50 years, it has been the joy of Kenneth Copeland Ministries to bring the good news to believers. Readers enjoy teaching from ministers who write from lives of living contact with God, and testimonies from believers experiencing victory through God's Word in their everyday lives.

Today, the *BVOV* magazine is mailed monthly, bringing encouragement and blessing to believers around the world. Many even use it as a ministry tool, passing it on to others who desire to know Jesus and grow in their faith!

Request your FREE subscription to the *Believer's Voice of Victory* magazine today!

Go to **freevictory.com** to subscribe online, or call us at **1-800-600-7395** (U.S. only) or **+1-817-852-6000**.

We're Here for You!

Your growth in God's Word and your victory in Jesus are at the very center of our hearts. In every way God has equipped us, we will help you deal with the issues facing you, so you can be the **victorious overcomer** He has planned for you to be.

The mission of Kenneth Copeland Ministries is about all of us growing and going together. Our prayer is that you will take full advantage of all The LORD has given us to share with you.

Wherever you are in the world, you can watch the *Believer's Voice of Victory* broadcast on television (check your local listings), the internet at kcm.org or on our digital Roku channel.

Our website, **kcm.org,** gives you access to every resource we've developed for your victory. And, you can find contact information for our international offices in Africa, Australia, Canada, Europe, Latin America, Ukraine and our headquarters in the United States.

Each office is staffed with devoted men and women, ready to serve and pray with you. You can contact the worldwide office nearest you for assistance, and you can call us for prayer at our U.S. number, 1-817-852-6000, seven days a week!

We encourage you to connect with us often and let us be part of your everyday walk of faith!

Jesus Is LORD!

Kenneth & Gloria Copeland

Kenneth and Gloria Copeland